Unique Pets

TARANTULAS

Kristin Petrie
ABDO Publishing Company

visit us at
www.abdopublishing.com

Printed in the United States of America, North Mankato, Minnesota.
052012
092012

 PRINTED ON RECYCLED PAPER

Cover Photo: Getty Images
Interior Photos: Alamy p. 7; AP Images p. 11; Glow Images pp. 15, 21; Heidi and
    Hans-Jurgen Koch/Minden Pictures/National Geographic Stock p. 9; iStockphoto pp. 5, 9, 12;
    Joel Sartore/National Geographic Stock p. 17; Photo Researchers p. 16; Thinkstock pp. 14,
    18–19; Thomas Marent/Minden Pictures/National Geographic Stock p. 13

Series Coordinator: Megan M. Gunderson
Editors: Megan M. Gunderson, BreAnn Rumsch
Art Direction: Neil Klinepier

Library of Congress Cataloging-in-Publication Data

Petrie, Kristin, 1970-
  Tarantulas / Kristin Petrie.
      p. cm. -- (Unique pets)
  Includes index.
  ISBN 978-1-61783-444-8
  1. Tarantulas as pets--Juvenile literature. I. Title.
  SF459.T37P48 2013
  595.4'4--dc23
                            2012011511

Thinking about a Unique Pet?
*Some communities have laws that regulate the ownership of unique pets. Be sure
to check with your local authorities before buying one of these special animals.*

CONTENTS

TARANTULAS

What has hairy, scary legs and makes people wary? It also has fangs and is a popular villain in movies. Many people scream when they see one! Yet others are taken by this creature's beauty. What kind of animal can be both feared and loved like this? It's the tarantula spider!

Tarantulas are arachnids from the scientific family Theraphosidae. This family includes nearly 1,000 spider species! Within this family are many popular pet tarantulas. These include the Mexican redknee, the greenbottle blue, and the Brazilian black.

Big, hairy spiders as pets? That's right! Tarantulas and their homes take up little space. They are inexpensive, hardy, and easy to take care of.

Although they look scary, many species are easygoing and gentle. Tarantulas give regular people just like you an opportunity to own a **unique** pet!

If you are afraid of spiders, you suffer from arachnophobia!

WHERE THEY LIVE

Where do these fascinating animals come from? Tarantulas are a diverse group of spiders, so they originate from equally diverse places! They live in warm areas on every continent except Antarctica. Some species live in very dry areas, while others live in tropical regions.

A tarantula's natural **habitat** determines the type of home it creates. Many tarantulas are ground dwellers. These spiders dig burrows in the soil. Other tarantulas are **arboreal**. They hang out in the natural **crevices** that occur in a tree's branches or bark.

Both ground-dwelling and **arboreal** tarantulas are known to line their homes with silk. They spin this silk from the spinnerets located at the rear of their **abdomens**.

Silk keeps tarantula burrows from collapsing and makes cozy pockets in the trees.

DEFENSE

A silk door and a trip line offer a tarantula protection from hungry predators. Vibrations on the silk alert the spider to approaching danger.

Lizards, birds, and snakes all find tarantulas to be tasty treats! But the tarantula hawk wasp may be the tarantula's worst enemy. It stings and **paralyzes** an unlucky tarantula. Then, it lays an egg inside the helpless spider. When the egg hatches, the spider becomes food for the baby wasp. Gross!

The tarantula's best defense is to stay hidden or to flee. If these options fail, the spider rears up on its hind legs or attacks with its large, sharp fangs.

For pesky predators, some tarantulas have a secret weapon. They use their rear legs to fling special hairs from their **abdomens**. These urticating hairs sting the predator's skin and eyes!

A tarantula flinging its urticating hairs

To humans, tarantula bites are similar to bee stings. They can be painful but are usually only dangerous if someone is allergic.

WHAT THEY LOOK LIKE

Like all spiders, the tarantula's body has two segments connected by a pedicel. The prosoma, or **cephalothorax**, is the first part. The top of this smaller segment features eight tiny eyes, the **chelicerae**, and the mouthparts. Eight legs and two **pedipalps** connect to the cephalothorax as well.

The second body segment is the opisthosoma, or **abdomen**. It houses the digestive, circulatory, reproductive, and respiratory systems. The abdomen ends with the spider's spinnerets. A tough **exoskeleton** covers the tarantula's entire body.

Tarantulas range greatly in color and size. Their bodies and hair can be black, brown, orange, blue, and even pink!

The largest tarantula species is the goliath birdeater. It can grow to about one foot (0.3 m) in length! It can weigh more than six ounces (170 g). Most species are much smaller. On average, they weigh one to three ounces (28 to 85 g).

A tarantula's common name, such as Mexican redknee, is often based on its colorful appearance.

BEHAVIORS

A foot-long, hairy spider is a scary sight to see! With their beady eyes and sharp fangs, even tiny tarantulas can be frightful. In addition, their slow movements look stealthy. Yet, these solitary creatures are **aggressive** only when they feel threatened.

A tarantula's eight eyes are grouped together on its cephalothorax.

Even though they have eight eyes, most tarantulas have terrible eyesight. Luckily, a strong sense of touch tells these spiders what is going on around them.

The hairs on a tarantula's body help it sense nearby objects. Silk helps, too! For example, uneven vibrations on its silk mean something is caught. On the other hand, smooth, regular vibrations might indicate rain.

The hairs on a tarantula's legs sense vibrations and odors.

FOOD

Tarantulas are carnivores, so they eat other animals. Yikes! But don't worry. As a human, you're safe! Common meals for wild tarantulas include insects such as grasshoppers, caterpillars, crickets, beetles, and cicadas.

In the wild, most of this feasting takes place at night. Tarantulas may hunt or just hide and wait for prey to pass by.

When the unsuspecting prey approaches, the spider springs to action! The tarantula grabs its prey and uses its fangs to **inject** the prey with **venom**. Unlike

Don't feed a new pet right away. Allow it to settle in for a week or so before providing its first meal.

14

most spiders, the tarantula's fangs move up and down instead of side to side.

In the wild, tarantulas may eat frogs or mice. However, these larger prey are not recommended for pets because they may cause an injury.

This bite kills small prey. And, it turns the prey's insides to liquid. Then, the tarantula sucks up the juices for its tasty meal. If the tarantula is not hungry, it will wrap its prey in silk to save for later!

Tarantula owners generally feed their pets crickets. Other insects and larvae can be included for variety. Young tarantulas will eat every 4 to 7 days. Older pets may only eat every 10 to 14 days. Just make sure fresh water is always available.

REPRODUCTION

Young tarantulas molt as often as once a month. Adults may only molt every one to two years.

Tarantulas mature slowly. They are not ready to reproduce until at least age three. Some wait until age nine! When ready to mate, a female emits **pheromones**. A male follows them to her burrow. There, he drums his feet to let her know he's arrived.

Then, the female has a decision to make. Do the vibrations mean predator, prey, or mate? An unlucky male may be eaten! But if the female decides to mate, the two spiders perform a courtship dance.

After mating, the female deposits up to 1,000 eggs in a silk cocoon she has made in her home. Then, she stands guard. After six to nine weeks, tiny spiderlings hatch.

Some spiderlings stay near their mother for a while, but others quickly scatter. Either way, many do not survive to adulthood. They are easy prey, and may even be eaten by their brothers and sisters!

Baby Antilles pink-toe tarantulas are blue. As adults, they are bright pink and green!

Those that survive will grow and **molt** throughout their lives. Males die shortly after mating. Females may live 25 years or more.

CARE

Have you decided you want a tarantula? Many different species are popular as pets. So one of your first decisions will be which type to adopt.

The first thing to consider is your experience as a pet owner. If you are a new tarantula owner, a spider with an easygoing temperament is the best choice.

Species such as the Mexican redknee are good choices for new tarantula owners. These slow-moving spiders do not mind being handled.

Species such as the orange baboon tarantula (OBT) are **aggressive**! In fact, some owners say *OBT* stands for "orange bitey thing"! These spiders are beautiful

Improper handling can easily injure your tarantula. A startled spider may jump from your hand and fall to the ground. Outside its home, your pet may get its claws caught in carpet or on your clothes.

to look at. But they are more likely to defend themselves with their fangs. They make good pets only for very experienced tarantula fans.

While tarantulas may become used to being held, their bodies are very delicate. Injuries from handling can result in death. Therefore, you should generally admire tarantulas from a distance.

THINGS THEY NEED

Once you have decided on your species, you will need to gather supplies. A ground-dwelling pet tarantula will be happiest in a small enclosure with soft **substrate** for burrowing. A tree-loving tarantula will enjoy a larger home with plants or branches for climbing.

Be sure your pet cannot escape its home. This will protect it from injury and from other pets. All species need an appropriate climate, too. Warmth and **humidity** are both important.

This may sound like a lot! But food, water, and a clean **environment** add up to a healthy tarantula. Healthy and happy tarantulas provide endless entertainment. Their mysterious behavior is fascinating to watch. Best of all, a pet tarantula can be a captivating companion for many years!

A tarantula's home should be kept away from direct sunlight.

GLOSSARY

abdomen - the rear body section of an arthropod, such as an insect or a spider.

aggressive (uh-GREH-sihv) - displaying hostility.

arboreal (ahr-BAWR-ee-uhl) - living in or frequenting trees.

cephalothorax (seh-fuh-luh-THAWR-aks) - the front body section of an arachnid that includes the head and the thorax.

chelicera (kih-LIH-suh-ruh) - either of the front, leglike organs of an arachnid that has a fang attached to it.

crevice - a narrow opening due to a split or a crack in something.

environment - all the surroundings that affect the growth and well-being of a living thing.

exoskeleton - the outer covering or structure that protects an animal, such as an insect.

habitat - a place where a living thing is naturally found.

humidity - the amount of moisture in the air.

inject - to force a fluid into the body, usually with a needle or something sharp.

molt - to shed skin, hair, or feathers and replace with new growth.

paralyze - to cause a loss of motion or feeling in a part of the body.

pedipalp (PEH-duh-palp) - either of the leglike organs of an arachnid used to sense motion and catch prey.

pheromone - a chemical substance animals release to signal others within their species. Pheromones help animals establish territories, attract mates, and warn of danger.

substrate - material such as moss or soil used to line the bottom of a tarantula's cage.

unique - being the only one of its kind.

venom - a poison produced by some animals and insects. It usually enters a victim through a bite or a sting.

WEB SITES

To learn more about tarantulas, visit ABDO Publishing Company online. Web sites about tarantulas are featured on our Book Links page. These links are routinely monitored and updated to provide the most current information available.

www.abdopublishing.com

INDEX